WALK WITH PURPOSE NOT ON PURPOSE

Transformation from Pain to Purpose

30 DAY DEVOTIONAL

T'KEYA ANN CORBIN

CONTENTS

DEDICATION

This book is dedicated to my son,
August Kirk.
Giving up will never be an option because of you!
I thank God for you daily. You changed me.

INTRODUCTION

I f I can be completely honest, this book came from a storm. I weathered it and I survived what I believe to be one of the roughest storms of my life.

A season where I was stripped of everything.

I lost my job, I moved into my grandmother's house with my 1-year old son, and I split from the one person I always believed was my life partner.

I was down to nothing. But sometimes being down to nothing is just the beginning of God working on you. A couple of months into this storm, I started writing...and writing...and writing. Slowly in 2017, this book began to take form It was an outlet. It was therapeutic. It was a place where I felt so free. It was my no judgement zone and reading my own writing helped me push pass the pain.

Once I began to get deeper, I realized this book was bigger than me! My relationship with God grew and I had my 'aha moment." It was in this act of obedience, God equipped me with insight, tools, prayers and a prophetic word *"Use what's in your hand and begin again!"*

Once I stopped asking God, *"Why me?"* and I began to say, *"God use me!"* it all became clear. I poured into this book all that I had during that storm. My emotions, my struggles, and a sense of transparency I had never experienced before. All so I could equip you with the proper tools you need to **_Walk in Purpose and not on Purpose_**. Life isn't just about existence, it's about truly living. Living up to the calling over your life.

If I did my job correctly, you will close this book understanding the grace of God and the things he can do to you and through you; if you open your heart and let him in to do the work. You won't be afraid to begin again. You will start to thrive in your purpose and begin to show up for yourself. Your prayer life will get stronger. If you are unclear about your purpose, it will be revealed to you all while preparing and aligning you with everything needed to carry out *His* vision.

I am determined to use my kind heart and uplifting words to encourage you to do the work.

Are you ready to be the best version of YOU internally and externally?

Are you ready to show up for YOU unapologetically?

Are you ready to see what can happen when you let God use 'what's in your hand' and focus on HIS vision?

Are you ready to see where life will take you?

If your answer is Yes to all of these questions, then this book is for you.

Let's begin!

DAY 1

OUR PLANS VS GOD'S PLANS

⁶ Then He said,"Hear now My words: If
there is a prophet among you,
*I, the L*ORD*, make Myself known to him in a vision;*
*I speak to him in a dream. ~**Number 12:6***

God makes no mistakes. We need to be thankful for everything he's done, everything he's doing, and everything that he is going to do! Have you ever prayed for something and months or maybe even years later thought back to that prayer and immediately had to thank God for letting that one go unanswered?

In those moments, you thought you were praying for the right thing but God said *"Those prayers are not in alignment with the things I have planned for your life."*

Imagine if God would have given you all the things you prayed for then, but you weren't prepared for it. We feel blessed when we receive an answer to our prayers and we need to be thankful for the unanswered prayers as well.

God knows best. He has the blueprint for our life-- just trust and believe Him. Even when bad things happen, you know God can bring the best out of a mess. It's not on your time. It's on God's time. We live in a generation where everyone wants microwave results.

When you cook a home cooked meal: you have to go to the store to get the items, unthaw meat, season the food, prepare, cook it, AND THEN you can sit down at the table and enjoy.

Just like the plans God has for you, He has to prepare you for it first. You must go hungry to hear a word from God, then he will place a vision on your heart. This vision will be aligned with your creativity.

Once that seed is planted down on the inside of you, He will prepare you to learn, grow, develop and obey until He feels you are ready to go to the next level.

Only God knows when you are ready for the blessings He has with your name on it. Remember that everything takes time. I want you to get out of the habit of thinking things are going to happen overnight because you won't do anything but disappoint yourself. Anything worth having doesn't come easy. If it did, you would feel like you could do it time and time again! It's when you put in the hard work, blood, sweat, tears, and prayers that you appreciate your blessings so much more.

Take your time. Stop trying to rush God's plans for your life. Be patient, pray, prepare for your blessing, process and progress. We are on God's timing. He's not on our clock. Just know whatever is meant for you will be just for you. Your blessings have your name on it already and no one can stop or block that!

DAY 2

WHO YOU ARE AND WHOSE YOU ARE

¹ O Lord, you have examined my heart and
know everything about me
.² You know when I sit down or stand up.
You know my thoughts even when I'm far
away.³ You see me when I travel
and when I rest at home. You know everything I do.
⁴ You know what I am going to say even before I say
it, Lord.⁵ You go before me and follow me.
You place your hand of blessing on my head.
⁶ Such knowledge is too wonderful for me,
*too great for me to understand! ~ **Psalms 139: 1-6***

God is always with you. He goes before you and makes your crooked paths straight. It's funny how even when you stress and worry about your current situation, everything ends up working for the greater good.

God's got you today, tomorrow and yesterday. His love for you will remain the same. God is our Father. He will never leave us nor forsake us. God's promise is God›s promise. You can stand on His word because His word never comes back void. It may take time to come to pass but be patient in the waiting season.

Know and understand the position God is calling for you to stand in. Don't go through life letting anyone use you but God. If you do so, you will always feel a void because life is about riding in the lane God has prepared for you only. Don't you dare let people impose their fears and insecurities on you --telling you who you are because of your past. Your past was a test which lead you to an amazing testimony.

Testimonies are powerful. Tell your story in a way that makes others comfortable to live in their truth. Don't do too much explaining. Let people think what they want about you. Usually the people talking about you are the people who don't know what they want out of life or where they are going. So shake it off and stand on it.

Take time to get to know you. Figure out what happiness looks like to you. Give yourself time to accept the new and improved you. Once God begins to change you, you will see the difference inside of you. You will begin to focus on all the good in you. Your mind will shift. The way you treat your body will be different. I once heard "*Your body is your personal vehicle through life. So you have to watch what gas you put in it and the fuel your using on it because you only get one car you can't trade it or change it so be careful with your car.*"

Loving people will become easy to you. It won't feel weird to receive love from strangers because some of these people are people God intended to cross your path. These people will help you in some way, shape, or form. You will begin to feel a sense of peace knowing that God got you behind the scenes. That feeling is amazing.

Finding a purpose is an unexplainable feeling especially knowing it came from God Himself. Surrender your *good idea* for **God's purposeful idea** even if that means taking a different route than you intended. Let God tell you who you are, not people. Let God lead you down the path of purpose and rightness. Don't let people lead you to a road of destruction.

Remember:

"*God can't bless who you pretend to be or who you compare yourself to! God only blesses a lane that was created for you!*"- Sarah Robert Jakes

DAY 3

GOD PEEL ME AWAY FROM ME

> *⁵ For when we were in the flesh, the motions of sins, which were by the law, did work in our members to bring forth fruit unto death. ⁶ But now we are delivered from the law, that being dead wherein we were held; that we should serve in newness of spirit, and not in the oldness of the letter. ~**Romans 7:5-6 KJV***

God strip me of me. I want to be made over. I am tired of being this person I thought I was. I am ready to learn the real me no matter the cost. I'll give up everything for I know your plans are greater than mine. Throughout the years I thought I knew who I was and where I was going but it landed me nowhere because they were my plans and not yours, Lord. My plans left me broken, empty, running and trying to fill voids that only You can fill. Once I received one touch of Your grace, I knew I had to run closer to you for your love. Your love is so fulfilling. It is so sweet.

This is my prayer to God. I know He's going to do the same for you if you let Him. The further you get, the more you realize the further you must go. God is going to remove toxic things out of you and make space for greater things to take place. When making room for the new don't fight it. Obey His commands for now you are in His hand.

You will learn the power of really letting things go because it's not your will. God knows what is best for you and what's not. Trust climbing this mountain to the top. It's not going to be easy. You must be willing to do the work. So many of us get lost in a world full of chaos. We dig deep inside of ourselves realizing there's nothing left because we've spread ourselves so thin. We give out all of our good stuff.

Have you ever gotten to a point in your life where you've asked yourself *"Who am I now?"* That's when you begin to want to know the real you. That's where it all started for me. I let God speak and begin to work on me. If you are currently reading this book, it says enough about you. It's time for you to let God peel you away from the you that you thought you knew; and make you over into the person you have the potential to be. I wish you the best of luck and no matter how hard it gets: never give up.

"You have greatness within you" - Les Brown

I want you to do the work, find a healthy balance, and let God use you in ways you never imagined. Give yourself time to think things through and process what is happening to you.

DAY 4

FORGIVENESS IS REQUIRED ON THE ROAD TO HAPPINESS

[14] For if you forgive other people when they sin against you, your heavenly Father will also forgive you. [15] But if you do not forgive others their sins, your Father will not forgive your sins. ~ ***Matthew 6:14 KJV***

How can you be happy if you are walking around holding a grudge? Holding a grudge against someone is like letting them live rent free in your head. If God forgives us for our sins, who are we not to forgive our neighbors? By holding that grudge, you are not hurting anyone but yourself. Holding onto grudges affect you internally. Bitterness has no benefit. If you hold grudges towards everyone that has wronged you, you won't have any room left for growth. This will cause you to be stuck right where you are.

The only person you are in control of is yourself. When a problem arises that doesn't sit right with you, let it out. Discuss it right there at that moment. Don't let time go by and don't talk about it with other people. I had to learn this the hard way: **you matter so express how you feel!**

If you don't want to address the problem right then and there, set up a date or a personal phone call. Do not, I repeat do not text how you feel because you can make matters worse. But it will live in your heart and that is not healthy. Address the problem, move forward and own it if you are in the wrong. Life is so much better when you love and let go. Happiness is a choice so is forgiveness. They go hand and hand. You must be willing to let go.

By doing so you are breaking strongholds off of your life. The devil would love for you to hold onto grudges forever. Once you release grudges and bitterness, you allow God to move in a way you have never seen. Forgiveness is just one stronghold you are breaking. Starting with one will lead you to breaking others holds such as: negative thinking, guilt, failure, and hopelessness.

You will feel clean inside. So do yourself a favor and clean yourself up (as well as others) and forgive. When you cleanse it doesn't always mean your body. Sometimes we need to cleanse our souls. Let go of the hurt from the past and make room for the new. To make room for the new you have to first throw out the old.

Start forgiving today.

DAY 5

CHANGE YOUR MIND CHANGE YOUR LIFE

> *Do not conform to the pattern of this world, but be*
> *transformed by the renewing of your mind. Then you*
> *will be able to test and approve what God's will is—his*
> *good, pleasing and perfect will.~ **Romans 12:2***

I always listen to motivational speakers, pastors, and successful people. The one thing they all have in common is: **once they changed their minds, they changed their life.** I didn't think much of the statement change your mind, change your life in the past. I never paid much attention to it until I was going through a storm. That storm made me change my way of thinking one day at a time. I simply started with the simple prayer *"Lord please change my mindset. My way of thinking is not aligned with what you have in store for my life!"*

Whether you know it or not: what you think or speak is what you are putting out into the Universe. To live out your dreams, you must first start with a vision. Then you have to create a plan. Once the plan is in place, create realistic goals that you can accomplish in a timely matter. Then as you follow the plan, you will then see your dreams manifest right before your eyes. It's hard to see your dreams clear with a cloudy vision and a lot of chaos going on around you. If you focus on all the wrong, how do you expect to get a breakthrough even when life doesn't seem fair? If you can just change your thinking, God will give you the ability to fix everything once you're in the right state of mind.

The first place the devil starts his work is the mind! It is the easiest place for him to attack. If he makes you feel stuck, he knows that you won't see where God is taking you. Don't fall into his trap.

When those negative thoughts come you, say, *"Devil I rebuke those thoughts."*

Starting now, I want you to live a life where you focus on the **solution** instead of the *problem*.

Here a few steps I took to develop positive thinking:

1. Stay in the word of God. First thing in the morning, read the Bible and thank God for waking you up instead of checking social media. Find a scripture to read and ask God how can I apply this to my life.
2. Listen to a sermon or a motivational speaker on YouTube. It will stir up something inside of you and inspire you to want to begin again.
3. Read at least 5-10 pages of a self-improvement book or something positive daily.
4. Surround yourself with positive people and start seeing the good in every situation.

DAY 6

FOCUS ON YOUR FOCUS

> *² Set your affection on things above, not on things on the earth.*
> *³ For ye are dead, and your life is hid with Christ in*
> *God. ⁴ When Christ, who is our life, shall appear,*
> *then shall ye also appear with him in glory.*
> *~ Colossians 3:2-4 (KJV)*

What is your focus? What is your why? What is your motive?

In life you should focus on something. Hopefully you are focusing on God's will for your life.

I pray that you are focused on your dreams and your life's purpose. When God created us, He created us with a purpose in mind. He knew our blueprint before we were formed in our mother's womb.

If you are not sure what your life's purpose is and want to find out: it's time to say YES to God and get as close to Him as possible.

He will lead you and not forsake you.

He will guide you through this journey of life.

He will give you a glimpse of your purpose.

He will build your character to prepare you for all that He has in store for you.

He will give you the tools that are needed to sit among the greats.

You must come to the realization that you are not living up to your full potential before you can begin walking in your destiny.

It's when you come into alignment for what God has planned for your life that you find out who you really are and what you were created to do.

Focus on the things that give you an overwhelming feeling, and focus on the calling God places on your heart time and time again!

It's time to shift your focus. What are you focusing on right now? Your life is a result of whatever it is you are focusing on. If you don't like what you are focusing on, it is time to move, adjust, change things around to bring everything into focus.

To focus means you must plan, prioritize, be obedient, make sacrifices, learn how to counsel with God and wait on His answer, create boundaries, work hard and expect miracles.

In the words of a wise man Les Brown, *"You don't have to be great to get started but you gotta get started to be great!"* Don't be afraid of starting over. It's never too late to create a new version of yourself.

Give birth and life to every God given idea that comes to you. Write it out. Set dates. Work on your goals daily.

*Invest in yourself and do it **NOW**! There are only so many tomorrows. If you're wondering when you should get started: there's no time like the present.*

DAY 7

DON'T SETTLE FOR SAFE

> *[18] "Do not remember the former things, Nor consider*
> *the things of old. [19] Behold, I will do a new thing,*
> *Now it shall spring forth; Shall you not know it?*
> *I will even make a road in the wilderness*
> *And rivers in the desert. ~**Isaiah 43: 18-19 KJV***

Uncomfortable situations will always be: well uncomfortable. But trust me, you'd rather be in an uncomfortable situation now (so you can be unstoppable later); than be comfortable now and stuck in the same spot forever.

When God is working on you it is not easy. But we must wait. Things get tough in the waiting season. God's maturing you and it's not going to feel normal.

When you know the purpose behind your "waiting season," you will keep going. God's granting you clarity. He can tell you your next move and how to go about it. Everything God wants you to have is right outside of your comfort zone. That's why you must have a strong mindset in your waiting season. To the untrained eye, it looks like you're struggling but you are in fact not. You look alone but you are not! God is right there coaching you and renewing you.

This season is not going to be easy. It's one step at a time. He has to shift things around in your life. He needs time to get rid of **people that you've been holding on to for too long** to make room for the **right people that are aligned with the places you are going** because you are going to need a strong team.

In this season, you will create new habits and get rid of the old habits holding you back.

The more you keep one foot in the past, the more it will delay you from the blessings in your future.

You are still in bondage to the past.

Let go of it.

Stop looking back.

You are not headed in that direction.

You've been living in the past for too long. You have to put it behind you. Move forward toward your destiny. God is going to give you vision, direction, and guidance with every step you take. You have to be willing to obey his word. Listen to his voice in the moments of stillness. Stillness is placed in your life to humble you but to mature you as well.

> *Today I want you to leave the past behind, clear*
> *your heart of the clutter and take hold of the*
> *glorious future God has planned out for you.*

DAY 8

NOT ALL STORMS ARE MEANT TO BREAK YOU

*⁷ Wisdom is the principal thing; therefore get wisdom: and
with all thy getting get understanding. ~ **Proverbs 4:7***

L earn to see the sunshine in the storm because every storm
comes with a message. Storms make you seek God harder and
that's why you are tested with one. In the midst of a storm, ask
God *what's my purpose* and He will show you. Your life will come
full circle.

But first you have to manage the storm you are currently in. Life's
storms come to give us what we lack. Whether it's strength, understanding, wisdom, knowledge, or guidance, it's what you need for
God to take you to the next level of life.

You should never come out of the storm the same way you went
in. God will break you down but He won't keep you at rock bottom.
He breaks you down to restore you and make you whole again. You
must learn to appreciate life no matter what season you are in. While
in this season, learn to take it one day at a time. Timing is everything.
God knows when you need that storm to come and wipe everything
away so you can have a fresh new start.

You're a survivor.
You'll gain back everything you lose.
God will restore you, heal you, and redirect you.
He will give you back everything the Devil tries to take from you.
Stay strong.
Remember people who helped you along the way.
Once the storm passes, tell your story. Wait for God's divine time
to tell your story.
Your story will help someone else through the same or similar

situation. This is a trying time in your life so you need to be with nourishing people who bring out the best in you.

Stay away from toxic people.

When God places a period in your life don't replace it with a question mark.

Life isn't about perfection it about progression.

You have to be willing to be okay and ready to fix those broken places.

When in life battles, you will change. You will be humbled and change your view on life.

Remember you're not in a bad place you are in the best place filled with God's grace over your life.

DAY 9

SCARS THAT ARE NOT THERE

> *⁵Casting down imaginations, and every high thing that exalteth itself against the knowledge of God, and bringing into captivity every thought to the obedience of Christ; ~ **2 Corinthians 10:5 (KJV)***

L ook in the mirror.
Look within.
Look deep within yourself.

What problems are you creating yourself?

Overthinking makes things seem worse than they are. Many of us are creating scars by holding on to past hurts.

Let it go!

We all are fighting battles. Don't create more for yourself by creating situations or living in the past.

Don't waste time wishing things are different.

Scars can also come from trying to live up to a superficial image. When trying to hold onto a false self image God can't properly use you. God needs you but first he needs the REAL YOU. Step out of that shadow that is scarring you. God is going to supply all your needs so stop looking at your empty hands saying *"I got nothing."* He is saying *"I have something that earth needs and I'm trusting in you to deliver it for me."*

Don't let the voices of society scar you. Remember you are building yourself. Don't downplay your growth. Don't limit your possibilities.

If you're anything like me you wonder *"Where do I fit in this world?"*

This is a world where everyone is living life through a phone screen.

We are lost in society.

Everyone wants to be tough and is living a lie.

People are holding on to an image.

Those are the real scars!

A lot of people today are feeling **worthless** because they are trying to be perfect by burying their authentic self instead of working for it.

People become materialistic to feel a sense of status. The crazy thing is that possessions don't make them happy. Once you put the phone down and take the designer clothes off, you are forced to face yourself. *How do I know all these things?* I was once that girl, too. But I was never okay with it.

I knew God couldn't bless who I pretend to be so I tapped into my authentic self.

Don't let the habits of your past or overthinking stop you.

Become a better version of yourself.

The change God has for you is not just for you. It's for the generations after you.

You will change the world when you let God use you.

Perfection is hindering you from living your best life.

Face your truth, embrace your truth and live your truth so that no one is able to use it against you!

And stop looking for the scars that are not there.

DAY 10

BATTLE OF CHOICES

For where your treasure is, there will your heart be also. ~Luke 12:34

Your mind thinks quickly. So if you don't pause to think on decisions, your mind will make choices that aren't the best for you. Your life is a result of your choices so you must choose wisely. Insecurity and fear play a big factor when making decisions but don't allow them to.

Remember that every action has a choice and a consequence. You have to be willing to accept both. When you learn to silence your mind and listen actively, decisions will be clearer because you can hear from God. He may not come to you in the moment you anticipate but move in a way that makes God say okay *"You are ready to hear what I have to say to you."*

Stop battling with yourself.

It's ok to wait.

You don't have to make instant decisions.

You can sleep on it.

It's better to not get other opinions because is can confuse you.

It's okay to ask for advice but the only voice you really need, other than yours, is God's voice.

Create solutions instead of making excuses.

DAY 11

YOU ARE WHAT COMES OUT OF YOUR MOUTH

From the fruit of their mouth a person's stomach is filled;
with the harvest of their lips they are satisfied.[21]
The tongue has the power of life and death,
*and those who love it will eat its fruit. ~**Proverbs 18: 20-21***

Y ou have not because you ask not.

You can speak brokenness into your life so watch what you say! It's easier to complain than be grateful for the things that you do have. Life can always be worse. If you think you have problems, God can show you someone with real problems.

Change your situation by changing your words.

Don't speak fear over your life speak faith into your life!

Watch what you say because it will manifest into your life.

Don't be afraid to go to God boldly for all the things you want but also listen to what God wants for your life too!

Make sure the things that are placed on your heart are Godly.

God has a way using you. So listen to Him so your wants and God's plans are aligned.

Start speaking things into existence. In the morning tell yourself *"Today will be a good day. Something good is going to happen to me today. I am a day closer to my breakthrough"* Start speaking life into dead situations. Stir those dreams up! Once you pray for the thing you want, go prepare for it. It may not come right away but if God promised it to you: it's coming in due time!

Stop getting in your own way by talking yourself out of the things you want.

You can not overcome what you won't confront.

Admit that YOU are the person that's been holding you back.

Every day is a new day.

Each day is a new beginning.

Create a new canvas and paint a picture of your life as clear as the vision God gives you over your life. Look at your situation and tell it I'm better than this! Beginning again. You have to be willing to do it God's way or no way! If you can't figure out your purpose then figure out your passion. Your passion will lead you to your purpose.

Make a U-turn, go uphill and follow the cross. It will lead to God's glory. Stop asking Him for the things you want and ask Him to make you how He wants you to be.

Now is your time to go from *"God why me?"* to *"God use me!"* He's been there and will show up for you. Are you willing to open up and ready to receive the things you've been praying for?

Prepare for the promises He has over your life!

DAY 12

You Owe It to Yourself to Focus on Yourself

*58Therefore, my dear brothers and sisters, stand firm.
Let nothing move you. Always give yourselves fully to
the work of the Lord, because you know that your labor
in the Lord is not in vain. ~ **1 Corinthians 15:58***

K now yourself.
     Learn yourself.
     Stand firm in what you want for yourself.
Work on yourself daily.

If you work 8 hours at someone else's company, then give least 1 hour to your own dreams or goals.

Your work for the Lord will always be rewarded. God places ideas and goals inside of you, so He wants to see those seeds manifest in due time. You must be willing to do the leg work. God will open new doors and bring new people into your life. You will meet people more like-minded. They will hold you accountable.

Create new habits.
Learn how to balance your life.
Have self-control.
Prioritize.
Be obedient.
Get organized.
Have self-discipline.
Create deadlines.
Hold yourself accountable.

Once you begin to work, you'll realize that God has an appointed time to fulfill the visions, dreams, and the desires of your heart. Take your time. You will grow with time. Taking your time doesn't mean procrastinate. It just means don't rush the process. Trust the process because the process is where you build character, confidence, strength, wisdom, standards, knowledge, commitment, time management, and boundaries.

Don't be so busy looking around at everything else that you lose focus on what really counts which is you. Your mission, your purpose and your destiny holds on to your faith.

Faith will help you push through life.

DAY 13

EVERY CHOICE YOU
MAKE, MAKES YOU

*⁴ Shew me thy ways, O LORD; teach me thy paths. ⁵ Lead
me in thy truth, and teach me: for thou art the God of my
salvation; on thee do I wait all the day.* ~ **Psalms 25: 4-5**

Once you start changing your life from the inside out, you
will be the change you want to see.

The clock is still ticking until it runs out.

If you are reading this then you still have time.

Quit trying to quit.

Don't give up on yourself before you even get started.

God marked you for greatness.

If you are going to be a world changer, you have to make better
decisions.

Pull yourself together and toughen up!

What you do in one season has major impact on your next season.

What you do today will determine what God does tomorrow!

You're right. I don't know what you have been through.

But stop using it as an excuse to keep you stuck.

You gotta check yourself. Trust me, you don't want anyone to do
it for you!

God will give you signs. Follow the correct road.

The hand of the Lord is on your life.

The choices you decide to make are up to you.

Where you are today is a result of the choices you made in the
past.

Ask yourself: *Am I happy with the life I am currently living?*

You must limit distractions so that you can tune into God.

Starve your distractions and feed your focus. So that you know the choices you make are aligned with God's plan for you.

We are human so we will slip and make ungodly decisions. When this occurs, don't walk around feeling guilty. God will forgive you and will help you make better decisions. God can still bless the mess you created.

If you are in an unhappy space in life, it is time for you to make better choices.

Choose wisely.

I encourage you today to get in alignment with God.

Take the time out of your busy day and add God to your schedule.

Pray in the middle of the day.

Worship.

Listen to a word from God.

Make God apart of your daily ritual.

Begin with this simple prayer:

God lead my life. Show me my purpose and my mission here on Earth. God change my mind because I know if you change my mind the rest will follow. Lord Jesus how can I walk and make decisions that are aligned with the season I am in? God remove anything and anyone helping me make poor decisions. God help me to understand myself. From this day forward Lord, I want to walk with a purpose and not walk on purpose.

Start saying that prayer everyday. The more you say it the more you will believe in it.

DAY 14

Take Time to Get in Touch with YOU

> *As each one has received a gift, minister it to one another, as good stewards of the manifold grace of God. [11] If anyone speaks, let him speak as the oracles of God. If anyone ministers, let him do it as with the ability which God supplies, that in all things God may be glorified through Jesus Christ, to whom belong the glory and the dominion forever and ever. Amen. ~ 1 Peter 4:10-11*

Do you know how important it is to know who you are and what you want out of life?

It's just as important to know that happiness can only come from you.

How can you expect someone to make you happy if you aren't taking on responsibility for your own happiness first?

You must know that everything you need God has already installed inside of you. Whether you get it from birth or from life lessons, remember you still have whatever you need inside of you. Now that you know those things STOP placing your happiness in the hands of someone else. People will leave you hurt, bitter, angry and disappointed the moment they do something that is not to your liking.

Getting to know yourself also means finding out what you like and dislike.

Once you get a sense of who you are and what you want, you will become unstoppable.

Your yeses will be a "Heck Yes!"

Your "No's" will be firm.

You have to sit down, humble yourself, date yourself and enjoy your own company.

Get comfortable with yourself and whatever someone else brings to the table will be extra.

If God's not bringing it, you will know instantly and you will return it back to the sender.

I've heard some words from a wise man John Gray. He said, "*The inner me can be my biggest enemy.*"

This means you when you fight with yourself you are holding yourself back. You are stopping yourself from being the best self.

Learn how to tame your mind.

You don't have to entertain those negative thoughts.

The more attention you give a negative thought the more you invite negative thoughts in your mind.

Let it go.

Meditate, do yoga or whatever helps you get in touch with your thoughts.

This way you can start to control your thoughts.

Set time aside and pray.

The more time you spend with God the more you will notice the change in your thought process. You can do all things through Christ who strengthens you. God places you here on Earth to do Kingdom work. It's time to stop settling because of your mindset.

*It's time to pray through the process and get
to work. God is depending on you.*

DAY 15

ALONE TIME IS NECESSARY

⁷Submit yourselves therefore to God. Resist the devil, and he will flee from you.⁸ Draw nigh to God, and he will draw nigh to you. Cleanse your hands, ye sinners; and purify your hearts, ye double minded. **~ James 4: 7-8**

Purpose will make you so focused. It will make you want to be alone to figure out who you are.

Time alone will let you **_see who God is._**
Time alone will let you **_see who you are_**.
Time alone will let you **_see what works for you._**

Starting over isn't always a bad thing.
It's a time for renewal.
Renewal is when God gives you a new view and new vision on life.
Don't run from it…
Face it, embrace it, and grace it.

Have no fear. Your process it not easy. It gets trying at times. It makes you want to run back to the familiar. It's much easier to go back to the things, people and places that you know than to stand alone in the season of transition. Do you know that your comfort zone is stopping you from getting to the level of elevation that God has for you?

The renewal process will cause you to lose long term relationships. Don't worry, it's all a part of the plan. Don't be afraid of losing people. Be more afraid of losing yourself trying to please people who don't even know who they are. If you place your values and happiness in the hands of someone else then you will always come up short. You will always feel like something is missing because it will always be a temporary fix. Once that moment is over you will still feel empty.

To fully be happy in life you must learn to love yourself and let God work on you in private.

Don't work for them (people). Work for Him (God).

When working for Him --peace, happiness, and prosperity will always follow.

Let people underestimate you so God can over qualify you.

No matter what they say keep on walking.

People can't take away who God created you to be.

Don't be satisfied with anything less than God's gifts for you.

God stamped you before you were created start acting like it!

There will always be somebody trying to stop you when you are living a life that pleases God. People won't understand the things you are doing because they can't see the whole picture. People will try to box you in. Don't let them.

When you allow the wrong people in your house, stuff will come up missing like joy, peace, love, hope and faith (*yes people steal these things if we allow them to*).

Watch the company you keep, stay at peace
and enjoy all of God's blessing!

DAY 16

GET WEIGHT OFF YOU!

Therefore, since we are surrounded by such a huge crowd of witnesses to the life of faith, let us strip off every weight that slows us down, especially the sin that so easily trips us up. And let us run with endurance the race God has set before us. ² We do this by keeping our eyes on Jesus, the champion who initiates and perfects our faith. ~ **Hebrew 12:1-2 (NLT)**

Feeling like the weight of the world is hanging over your shoulder is the worst feeling ever.

It feels like life is coming at you from all angles.

It's uncomfortable.

You are faced with ongoing battles one after another.

You feel like you're drowning underwater and you need to come up for air.

You feel like no one feels your pain.

Trust me we've all been there before. A lot of us are fighting similar battles. We are just too afraid to speak up because we feel as if we will be judged.

You feel like you're surrounded by a lot of people, but no one gets you or see you.

You keep playing out the storm in your head day in day out.

You keep thinking about what part you played to deserve this!

Ask God to help you make the right choices so that you can see the clear skies and rainbows on the other side of this storm. Your storm is only temporary; temporary is never forever. When you feel overwhelmed, you are letting what's going on outside get inside of you! Learn to fight these battles in prayer and worship. God will fight your battles for you. Just be patient, sit back and watch Him work. He didn't say you won't be under attack.

He said "No weapon formed against you shall prosper." *Isaiah* **54:17**
He said "All things work together for good" *Romans* **8:28**.

So learn to embrace the storm. Once it's over, let the rain wash you clean of guilt, shame, sins, lies, materialism, greed, fear and jealousy. God didn't let you endure pain, so you can go back to the same person you were before the pain. No, no, no. He let you go through Hell, so you can have a peace that nothing or no one can disturb.

He wanted you to learn to wear your spiritual eyes and take your faith to the next level. At this point you should understand that God has a purpose for your life. Remember what didn't kill you made you stronger. Now it's time to pray, prepare and work. You should have nothing weighing you down. God took care of that. You have to pack light to where God is taking you. Don't get offended when people you thought were in this life journey with you begin to disappear. This is God's work.

Be open.
Let God use you in a way to help others.
Be bold.
Tell your story.
Live your truth and no one can ever use it against you.
The bigger the storm the bigger the purpose.
Sometimes victory is not going to always look pretty or perfect.
Know that you are carrying something valuable so stop talking yourself out of your miracle.
Life happens to all of us.

Are you going to dwell on the past or let God
turn that mess into a message?

DAY 17

PEOPLE CAN BE A DISTRACTION
FEED YOUR FOCUS

*[7] "Ask and it will be given to you; seek and you will find; knock and the door will be opened to you.~ **Matthew 7:7***

D on't be so caught up in the world around you, that you forget to live your own life. Living your own life requires you doing what works for you! In this day and age it's so easy for you to get consumed and caught up looking at everybody else's life on television, reality shows, blogs and YouTube.

You can find yourself over analyzing your life.

You may feel like you're not doing enough.

You may feel like you should be further ahead then you are now.

Jealousy may begin to arise.

You may find yourself getting mad at other people's accomplishments.

You may feel as if your life is at a stand still but in reality you are right where God wants you to be. Your timing isn't the same as everyone else's. It's called **YOUR TIME** for a reason. Don't compare someone else's season with your season.

You may have to struggle for a few years but in that struggle you are able to build character, learn to obey, learn to prioritize, manage your time and manage your finances. Hard times are when you find all the tools you need for where God is taking you. We serve a supernatural God. What may seem like a struggle is actually an assist. Struggle sets you up for your greatest accomplishment. What takes someone three years to do, God can do for you in three months when it's *YOUR TIME.*

Recognize that some people are moving but not going anywhere because they are moving in the wrong direction. So don't envy someone else's journey.

You have to go through the season of loss to gain all you need.

Your destiny has a timeline of its own and only God knows when it is your time.

So wait patiently and while waiting learn to celebrate along the way!

DAY 18

REAL FRIENDS

Be not deceived: evil communications corrupt good manners. ~1 Corinthians 15:33

[33] *Be not deceived: evil communications corrupt*
good manners. ~**1 Corinthians 15:33**

I t's time to reevaluate your friends.

Don't use the term so freely.

Be protective of your space, your heart and energy.

Your friends should be pouring into you what you are pouring into them.

They should be holding you accountable for your actions, goals and words.

The people you surround yourself with help to build and shape you.

Friends should be there in good times and bad.

They weather storms with you.

Friends don't talk about you as soon as you turn your back.

I need you to understand that some people are only in your life for a reason or season. Everyone's not meant to last a lifetime. Learning who is in your life to nourish you is important. These are the people that will bring the best out of you and see things in you that you can't see in yourself.

Leave toxic friendships behind. Toxic people will drain you and make you feel bad about wanting more out of life. Toxic people expect you to stay the same. Take inventory of who has access to you. If you don't know which friends are nourishing or are toxic, create a list of pros and cons for each friend. If the bad outweighs the good: it's time to let that friend go!

Ask yourself:

• Does this friend celebrate me? Do they support my dream?

- Is this friend using me?
- Does this friendship make me better?

I know you're probably thinking *"I've known this person forever. I can't just stop being their friend."* Yes you can! You will find some of your best friends in your adult years because you are more developed. As an adult, you will better know what type of people you want to surround yourself with.

When people are growing in different directions it's usually best to part ways. It's time to let friends go when they begin to say *"You think you're better than me."* You're not better than anyone. Sometimes you are simply better off without them. I mean that in the most humble way! Be great. If you get shaded on the way it's ok.

Keep climbing to the top because the bottom is crowded.

DAY 19

WE RISE BY LIFTING
EACH OTHER UP

> *[11] Therefore encourage one another and build each other up, just as in fact you are doing.[12] Now we ask you, brothers and sisters, to acknowledge those who work hard among you, who care for you in the Lord and who admonish you. [13] Hold them in the highest regard in love because of their work. Live in peace with each other.* ~*1 Thessalonians 5:11-13*

Instead of judging and knocking people down, ask how you can help with something. We have enough people in the world beating each other down. Try treating people how you want to be treated.

We are all fighting.

Some of us are fighting the good fight of faith.

Some of us are fighting our own battles.

Some of us are fighting battles in our heads.

We are all fighting something behind closed doors. So there's no need to fight each other. We all want the same thing out of life peace.

Plus, you never know who you can come across or strike up a conversation with. First impressions always have a major impact. So treat the janitor with the same respect as the CEO.

Don't be afraid to let people know how you feel about them! Don't take the good people in your life for granted. Let them know you admire them and what you gain by having them in your life or in your circle. Learn who you can walk with and who you should keep at a distance. You need to pack light for the level of elevation that God is taking you to!

If people can't celebrate you now they can't reap the benefits with you later. If you aren't able to identify these people, ask God. Ask Him to give you insight on the intentions of the people around you. Ask God if the friends you have now are good for you. If they are not, ask God to remove them and replace them with people that will add value to your life.

We were placed here to serve one another.

We all have the gift to touch another life with our story, our talents, or the opportunities we share.

Help people around you realize what they are good at.

Point out the things that you see in them that they can't see in themselves.

Give advice.

Take advice and really apply it to your life.

It doesn't cost anything to give a compliment. So give them freely.

Once you are in touch with your light you won't try to dim anyone else's.

In fact, your light within will give women the courage to light their own light.

Ask God to use you in a way to help others in any way possible.

Don't envy anyone else's life because of the things you see. You only see a glimpse.

No one is perfect. Be happy in real life.

Don't strive to be what you see on the internet.

We don't all have the same blueprint but God has great plans
for each of us. Alone you can go fast, together you can go far!

DAY 20

Fill Other Cups without Leaving Yourself Empty

> *⁴ There are different kinds of gifts, but the same Spirit distributes them. ⁵ There are different kinds of service, but the same Lord. ⁶ There are different kinds of working, but in all of them and in everyone it is the same God at work.~ **1 Corinthians 12:4** (NIV)*

L end a helping hand. What is it going to take away from you to help someone in need?

Lending a helping hand betters you when it's done from the heart.

Giving with a heart of grace should always be an easy task.

Don't help people expecting a favor in return. Help people with a pure heart.

To be successful, you must be willing to help people and let people help you.

God determines your greatness by how many people you serve not by the people you boss around. A great leader was once a servant. Great leaders will get in the game and get dirty if needed. Great leaders set an example and show you how to get it done the right way. A boss can show you the game but a leader can change your life. We live in a generation where everyone is self-made and independent. But to be honest, that's not the right way to go through life.

Alone you can get things done fast. But are getting things done fast, more important than getting it done right?

Each successful person you meet will always have a team.

It's important for you to bring what you know to the table then feed off the help and the support of others.

Together we can go far.

God always place people in our lives to help us whether we want to acknowledge it or not.

Start your day with God then ask Him, *"How can I help someone today?"*

The smallest deed can get you far.

Holding the door, sparking up a conversation or simply smiling at someone can make someone's day.

Leadership and serving go hand in hand.

Teach the things that you learned. It can be a blessing to someone. That same person you are teaching can teach you.

Everyone can drop gems. Always look for a lesson in your daily interactions.

Every position you were placed in, every job you took, and every experience was for you to serve in the Kingdom. Life prepares you for the big thing God has in store for you. You needed that extra skill set to go that extra mile.

Take pride in helping others because while you are helping others you are truly helping yourself.

DAY 21

FROM BROKEN TO BEAUTY

⁷The law of the LORD is perfect, converting the soul: the testimony of the LORD is sure, making wise the simple.⁸ The statutes of the LORD are right, rejoicing the heart: the commandment of the LORD is pure, enlightening the eyes.⁹ The fear of the LORD is clean, enduring for ever: the judgments of the LORD are true and righteous altogether. ~Psalms 19:7-9(KJV)

L ife has a funny way of dealing its cards.

A picture can say a 1000 words or 1000 lies.

Don't be foolish and get caught up with social media that it makes you afraid.

Don't think the things you want out of life will be handed to you based on what you see on Instagram.

Don't be a person with a house full of things but you're still empty.

Looking from the outside in your life can look perfect. But a perfect life can leave you broken.

A perfect life is sometimes missing peace, love, and happiness.

If you're not rooted in God's foundation, you will always feel like something is missing.

Until you give yourself all of you, you will never get to experience all the beauty God has stored for you.

You are so much more valuable than anything you own.

God created a lane just for you.

I used to be caught up in appearances. I wanted everything I saw. I wanted new bags and trips. I thought I would be living the dream with material things. I finally had all the material possessions. I looked good on the outside and was broken on the inside. I was dealing with low self-esteem, negative thinking, mental abuse, and control issues. I allowed a man to break me because he was able to provide the life I thought was a dream.

The big house, nice cars, vacations and luxury things didn't stop me from crying each night.

I cried out to the Lord at night not knowing where things went wrong. I would always pretend everything was ok but most of the time it wasn't true. I would post perfect pictures but I never had a peace of mind. I finally got to a point in my journey where I started to battle within myself.

I wanted true happiness even if that meant sacrificing everything.

I had to let go of the superficial.

I knew I had to obey God and do whatever he was telling me to do if I wanted truth peace on Earth.

I suggest the same! It's time.

Give yourself time to grow.

Let go of anything that is keeping you from knowing your worth.

Step up and into who you really are.

Connecting to yourself is far more important than any material thing or accomplishment.

Your inner life will always be amazing once you know who you are.

Do the work that is needed inside before trying to upgrade your life outside.

Pray this simple prayer today:

Lord I know you can't bless who I pretend to be. So peel back the layers. Remove the old version of me and create who I am supposed to be. Take what you need to take away and give me what I need so that I can be the best version of myself and lead others to you with my life and love. Amen

DAY 22

THE COMEBACK IS ALWAYS STRONGER THAN THE SETBACK

> [24] *The LORD is my portion, saith my soul;*
> *therefore will I hope in him.*
> [25] *The LORD is good unto them that wait for*
> *him to the soul that seeketh him.*
> [26] *It is good that a man should both hope and quietly wait*
> *for the salvation of the LORD.* ~ ***Lamentations 3:24-26***

Do not spread yourself so thin.

Don't say "*Yes*" to everyone but yourself.

It's okay to put yourself first. (Yes even before your kids).

If you can't be fully happy with yourself, how are supposed to make the people in your life happy?

Being completely happy with who you are is very important.

Look in the mirror.

Talk to yourself.

Tell yourself you are beautiful.

Don't wait around for someone to take you on a date. Date yourself.

Set some standards.

Have some morals.

Hold yourself up to high expectations!

Don't settle.

Don't be afraid of speaking your mind or addressing a conflict when it arrives.

Women in relationships, don't be so caught up in loving a man you forget about yourself.

You matter.

People look for your weaknesses and flaws and try to use them against you. Don't let them.

Love yourself so you can show people how to love and treat you.

Don't feel bad about setting standards, creating bounties, and being confident.

Only insecure people will feel offended when you begin focusing on you. Like-minded people will understand.

Self-discovery is one of the many things money can't buy!

If you don't have confidence in private you won't have power in public.

Stand firm in believing in yourself.

Fear is another thing that can rob you of your joy.

Let your cup overflow with faith so that you are able to kick fear out and get your happiness back. Stop letting fear talk you out of your dreams. Only you can stop you from getting things done. People make excuses for the things that don't want. People make the things they want happen. Stop thinking *"This isn't supposed to be happening to me"* every time something doesn't go as planned.

If you know who you are then you know who you are not. People today are going through an identity crisis because they don't know who they are and what they want out of life.

To discover who you are, ask yourself:

- What's down in my soul?
- What is my motivation?
- Do I have self-discipline?

> *Tap into your core beliefs. I don't want you to be the person that can fix everyone's life but your own!*

DAY 23

IF YOU WANT IT BAD ENOUGH, FIGHT FOR IT

*[25] Everyone who competes in the games goes into strict training. They do it to get a crown that will not last, but we do it to get a crown that will last forever. ~ **1 Corinthians 9:25 NIV***

At the center of every dream, every goal, every strength, every breakthrough, and every success story is a person with self-discipline.

How can you obtain the life you really want to live without self-discipline?

You can't. It's impossible.

You have to train your mind and yourself to make the best decision based on what God's promise for you.

We have freedom but as an adult you have to hold yourself accountable for your actions.

Self-discipline isn't something you're born with. So once you identify that you lack

self-discipline, it's time to work on it.

The last thing you want to be in life is someone with no self-control.

Those types of people have nothing but a bucket of excuses.

Excuses build bridges to nowhere.

Take baby steps to improve.

This is a lifelong change so don't expect it to happen overnight.

When you feel the road is getting rough pray and ask God how to overcome.

Keep track of your progress.

Create a list of priorities.

Try to get as organized as possible.

Set boundaries and motivate yourself by adding something positive to your daily ritual.

Motivation will sometimes die. That's when self-discipline is important. Walking by faith is even more important in these moments. You must be willing to stand on God's word. God needs to see you consistently praying, planning and working. Remember that prayer without works is dead.

It's amazing what you can accomplish when you don't get in your own way.

You are capable of doing all the things God has called you to do. It's going to require hard work and dedication.

You should already have a plan set up for you.

If you don't have one now then it's time to create one.

Pay attention to your focus, spending, eating and mindset.

Remember self-discipline and balance go hand and hand.

God also wants to see that you are obedient and faithful with the little things in your life before he can bring the overflow.

Trust me overflow is coming your way.

Your time is now.

So get out of that self-doubt and step into self-disciple.

It's time to take ownership of your life.

Sacrifice now so later you won't be living with regret.

Watch how you are spending your time.

The enemy knows he can't destroy you, so he will try his best to keep you distracted.

He will do anything to derail our destiny. He brings doubt and confusion so that we are not able to focus.

It's time to stir up that fire again. No more excuses.
Make up your mind and keep going.

DAY 24

THE GREAT ESCAPE

*² Be watchful, and strengthen the things which remain, that are ready to die: for I have not found thy works perfect before God.- **Revelation 3:2 KJV***

Feeling stuck is one of the worst feelings in life. We daydream to escape our current circumstances when we don't like it. We plan to escape our daily routines with a vacation to somewhere beautiful. We want to escape all the hardships, rumors, hurt, and pain. It gets trying when you want to escape bondage and addiction. You often feel trapped and we just want to be free. Free from everything that is disrupting your peace and sanctity.

The true definition of the great escape here on Earth is submitting and surrendering yourself to God. I'm here to tell you: **YOU** must be willing to do the work to reach the great escape. Let Him guide and take your life by the hand. You have to dig deep within yourself, address your problems and give them to God and leaving them there!

What does it mean to be free? It's living a stress-free life knowing God is in control of everything. Digging deep can cause some hurt.

If you have places that are too dark, see a therapist.

With therapy you can address questions you have about yourself or your childhood.

You can finally talk about those dark places and finally let everything out.

You have to remove yourself of anything that causes you to go back to any dark places.

Limit your to the television shows you watch that can be a trigger.

Watch who you speak to.

Watch what you say.

This is your trial and error season. You will feel tested. Apply the lessons to your everyday life. If you don't get it right the first time, it's okay. You can try again. Be mindful and don't get mad when people hold you accountable for your actions.

You will realize the further you go the further you have to go. The season leading to the great escape is not easy. If you get there beaten, broken, busted and bruised just know that God will be right there waiting on you.

Let that light at the end of the tunnel keep you going.
Each step is a step closer to breakthrough.
It's such an amazing place.
It will be worth it.
Watch how your life will come full circle.
It will all work out.
The good, bad, ugly and amazing fits into God's plan for your life.
It's all going to turn out right.

DAY 25

FULL CIRCLE

> *¹⁷ The righteous cry, and the* LORD *heareth, and delivereth them out of all their troubles.*
> *¹⁸ The* LORD *is nigh unto them that are of a broken heart; and saveth such as be of a contrite spirit.*
> *¹⁹ Many are the afflictions of the righteous: but the* LORD *delivereth him out of them all. ~ **Psalms 34: 17-19***

Nothing that you have been through is a mistake or isn't worth it! Everything happens for a reason. Even the pain. When we're in our season we may not understand it, but know that purpose and pain go hand in hand.

No matter where you are in life right now begin to thank God.

Whether you are going through a season of hardship or a season of all praise *give thanks*. You are better than good (and some days greater than that).

You've come too far to go back.

In life you will receive a glimpse of your dream.

You are who God is preparing you to be before even getting to where God is taking you.

Life experiences grow you up.

It builds character so you won't forget where you come from.

Don't let go of your dreams.

Dig deep and remember God can make miracles out of mistakes.

Don't let the naysayers get in your way. The enemy will use people to knock you off course.

Life is funny. It may look like you took a turn in the wrong direction but in reality, it's just a detour. You're still in route, so stay on course.

We are faced with life detours daily such as fear, worry, stress, insecurities, anxiety, relationships, bad breakups, toxic friendships, and childhood pains. These are things the enemy will try and throw on your road towards destiny. God never said it was going to be an easy trip.

Your destiny is right outside of your comfort zone. Stepping out of your comfort zone isn't an easy task. You've got to let God take the lead on this one. That's what it means to walk by faith. When walking in faith you can't let those thoughts of fear distract you.

Before starting this journey, you must build up your faith. When a thought of fear comes to mind say, *"Devil I rebuke you and I'm standing on the word of God he will never leave me nor forsake me!"*
Faith and fear **cannot coexist**.
The only thing stopping you from being the best version of you is your fear of failing. So today overcome that fear.

> *Get in your car of faith and start on your journey to a purpose filled life that will lead you to your destiny.*

DAY 26

REBIRTH

> *God saved you by his grace when you believed. And you*
> *can't take credit for this; it is a gift from God. ⁹ Salvation is*
> *not a reward for the good things we have done, so none of us*
> *can boast about it. ¹⁰ For we are God's masterpiece. He has*
> *created anew in Christ Jesus, so we can do the good things*
> *he planned for us long ago. ~**Ephesians 2: 8-10 (NLT)***

Have you noticed that women experience hurt, pain and suffering after giving birth to a baby? That experience is a REBIRTH. That pain could be a divorce, separation, loss of a job, house, car, money, bad break up, death, rape, or neglect.

When you're fighting, and you have your hands up in front of you that's all you are able to see. You can't see clearly with your hands up in front of you. When you're in a position to fight not just physical you have your guard up mentally as well, you aren't thinking clearly.

A rebirth causes us to look in the mirror and readjust our crown. Once the smoke clears, put your hands down and look around at life from a different perspective. Your hands are down now you will begin to see things clearer and brighter. You will notice things that you never noticed before. God will allow you to see yourself properly once you surrender to Him in every area of your life.

Rebirth requires a different you.

Don't forget about all the hurt and the pain you have been through.

Take all that with you.

Understand that will create a stronger you.

Tell your story with no guilt, shame, or insecurity.

You will then begin to notice what you were once fighting.

Life will begin to work for you.

Embrace your story.

During your rebirth, you will live free, open and unapologetic. You will begin to see and move up to a new level that has your name on it. Happiness will be a priority! Show up for yourself. Check in with yourself daily before pouring into another's cup. People around you will treat you differently because they see you treating yourself properly. Self-worth is more than self-care. Knowing who you are brings on a different type of respect.

Self-worth is a very important part of your rebirth!

Start viewing yourself the way God sees you and you will be unstoppable.

Go after His plans for you.

Peace will come easily.

Joy will come easily.

Love will come easily.

God provides you with it all when you are flowing in the stage of rebirth.

He knows you want more.

He sees you showing up for yourself so he will provide.

Nobody is as good at being you than you.

Get out of your own way.

Shake off the old.

Let go to bring forth the REBIRTH in you.

DAY 27

FRESH START

Even the youths shall faint and be weary,
And the young men shall utterly fall,
[31] But those who wait on the LORD Shall renew their strength;
They shall mount up with wings like eagles, They shall run and
not be weary, They shall walk and not faint. ~Isaiah 40:30-31

Ask God, "*What do You want me to do?*"
Ask God, "*What do You have for my life?*"

Start seeing yourself as the best version of yourself.

Learn how to use your current circumstances to your benefit.

Reflect on your past and learn to let it go. In order to become the person God is calling you to be, you must let the person you once were die.

Remember that people, places and things have expiration dates so never place a question mark where God placed a period.

When going through this transition a lot of changes will occur.

The changes are necessary for your growth and development process.

Remember that people come into your life for a reason, seasons, or a lifetime. So people will fall out of your life. Don't dwell on it. The next level will bring you new friends, new opportunities, new missions, new blessings, and a new insight on life.

You can't settle for safe. The things you want in life, your dreams and desires are outside of your comfort zone. So change your mind to change your life.

Start seeing yourself in a different light.

Every day you wake up is a new opportunity to do better, be better and lead a better life. It is going to be a fight, but you have to be willing to put on the armor of God and go to **war.** Your place of purpose needs you to take your position. It may seem easier to live your old life but commit to the person you're becoming.

You must commit to your vision and stay committed *during the good and the bad*. Greatness doesn't happen overnight. Slow progress is better than no progress.

> *If you want your transformation bad enough you have to fight for it work day and night for it.*

DAY 28

CELEBRATE YOU

*25 She is clothed with strength and dignity, and
she laughs without fear of the future.
26 When she speaks, her words are wise, and
she gives instructions with kindness.
27 She carefully watches everything in her household
and suffers nothing from laziness.~ **Proverbs 31:25-27***

Stop being afraid of YOU!

Don't wait for someone else to pat you on the back, BE PROUD OF YOU.

You did it.

You made it this far with the grace of the Lord over your life.

Give yourself credit when no one is clapping for you!

You are free.

Free of all the guilt, shame, negative self-talk, misjudgment, abuse, and negative thinking. Finally, you can see yourself again for all that you are.

It's time to WIN.

Learn that nobody is going to take care of you like you will take care of you.

The love you crave so badly from someone else, learn to give it to yourself first.

Learn to unpack you so you can rise to the next level God is calling you to.

Being called beautiful and feeling beautiful are two totally different things.

Start looking in the mirror and acknowledging you.

Stop seeing yourself from the same point of view. It's a new you.

You're not the same. *You lost that weight, you've changed your ways, you cut your hair, you've improved.*

It's time to realize it.

It's ok to compliment yourself and wear a smile on your face.

Because you remember those days you couldn't stand to see your own face in the mirror.

Wake up with joy on your heart knowing you're not so hard on yourself anymore.

It's hard trying to fit into places you didn't belong.

It's hard pretending to be somebody EVERYBODY wants you to be.

It's ok to take care of yourself, date yourself and figure out what happiness looks like to you.

The truth is what made you happy when you were pretending will not make you happy when you discover your real self within.

It your time.

Don't let anyone tell you any different.

You will discover the life you truly want to live
but to live that life you must be authentic.

DAY 29

FAITH IT UNTIL YOU MAKE IT

Who are kept by the power of God through faith unto salvation ready to be revealed in the last time.⁶ Wherein ye greatly rejoice, though now for a season, if need be, ye are in heaviness through manifold temptations: ⁷ That the trial of your faith, being much more precious than of gold that perisheth, though it be tried with fire, might be found unto praise and honour and glory at the appearing of Jesus Christ.
~1 Peter 1:5-7

Faith it until you make it! When stepping out in faith you're not going to be comfortable. In life, God sometimes will strip us of everything so you can understand what's going on around you. God is going to take the fear out of you. For Him to do so you must be willing to face your fears. Remember God is bigger than your fear. When you step into fear or feel it arriving, continue to push yourself into faith. Rest in God's words and His promise for your life.

Know that God will make a way out of no way.

Life is not perfect but it's not worth faking it. Faking it requires too much energy. You pretend to be someone you're not rather than the person He created you to be.

God said *I want to grow you up.*

To grow you have to face all the areas in your life that you are too ashamed to show the world.

Stop lying to yourself.

The mirror doesn't have a filter.

Take all the makeup off.

It's time to face those areas in your life that are not so glamorous but that are faithful. It's not about perfection, it's about progression.

The moment you come to the realization that your image isn't everything, *the better off you will be.*

To make it to the next level of life, you have to be willing to leave the person you thought you were.

Understand God will break you to make you whole again.

It's a rebirth.

You will go through a season when you don't feel like yourself. It's going to be very awkward.

You will feel alone in this season.

This season is going to be just you and God.

I suggest watching how you spend your time. When I was in this season I created new habits of reading the Bible and self-improvement books. I placed meaningful scripture on little note cards and placed them in my purse or wallet. In discouraging moments, I would dwell on the word of the Lord. After this season you will find yourself in a place of peace. It's going to feel amazing.

When you're in this season:

1. Listen. Don't listen to respond but listen with your heart. Listen so you can hear God's voice.
2. Ask God who you should remove and keep in your life. (When walking in your purpose you need to be in good company!)
3. Wait on clarity and confirmation from the Lord when it's time to move

"Your team knows your dreams, your tribe knows your vibe, your crew understands what you been through"- John Gray

DAY 30

It's Time to Build Your House

> *I am about to build a Temple to honor the name of the LORD my God. It will be a place set apart to burn fragrant incense before him, to display the special sacrificial bread, and to sacrifice burnt offerings each morning and evening, on the Sabbaths, at new moon celebrations, and at the other appointed festivals of the LORD our God. He has commanded Israel to do these things forever. **2 Chronicles 2: 3-4(NLT)***

To learn yourself, you have to be willing to unlearn some unhealthy habits. Each day God is giving us more and more responsibility for our journey. This requires us to build our house. To be honest, building your house is going to require you to face a lot of truth about yourself which can be hard to do.

Here are the stages that you will go through.

<u>Step 1: Ground Zero or Rock Bottom (Demo Day).</u> This is the place where you experience the most damage. You will start to feel tired of your old life. This is where your initial change begins. Rock bottom can be a storm of some sort. It can be dealing with the loss of a family member, a bad break up, financial difficulties, legal issues, or depression. Ground zero is when you look in the mirror and you don't even know who you are. Each and every last one of us has been at rock bottom.

<u>Step 2: Doing The Internal Work (Laying Your Foundation).</u> Internal work is extremely hard and it's not for the weak. First you hurt then you heal. You must be willing to face the painful truth about yourself if you're going to create a better you. You must face the areas you thought only you can see!

Keep a journal of this process.

This will require you to get closer to God to see yourself clearer than before.

Laying your foundation requires you to tell the truth to yourself like never before.

Love yourself properly so you can exceed in what's next for you.

For me this required celibacy because I didn't know how to balance being in a relationship and work on me. I had to give me all of me!

Laying your foundation will have you doing things like creating a budget, breaking bad habits, realizing what you like and don't like about yourself, and your boundaries.

This process requires a lot of homework. Are you willing to do the assignments? God will be grading you since He's the teacher. If completed right, you will have self-respect, morals and standards (if you don't already have some).

If done properly this will even have you looking at yourself in the mirror asking, *"Do I know this person?"* with a smile on your face.

You will be able to look in the mirror and not see pain.

You won't need anyone to tell you they will see your growth.

You will see your worth because you will know who you are and whose you are (A Child of God).

This isn't a process that will happen overnight. You didn't become the way you are overnight. It takes time, so be patient. Remember that the more you grow, the more you have to learn. Keep that in mind, this isn't a test you take and get right on the first try,

This is a lifetime test.

Once you pass one test and God takes you to the next level, trust me another test is coming.

New levels require different versions of you and God needs to know He equiped you properly from the prior test that life put you through.

Step 3: Creating Boundaries and Setting Priority (Framing). Learn who's here for a lifetime, reason and season. Some people were placed in your life for a reason or season. Don't hold on to them for a lifetime position. To soar, you have to let them go. Break free of those chains.

Setting boundaries teaches people how to treat you. Stop trying to fix everyone's problem because you can't fix anyone. Fix **yourself**.

When setting boundaries you must be very honest with people and use your time wisely. Don't let people suck you of your energy. You need all your energy to do great things and do the work of the Lord. In this stage pay attention to signs. God will show you who's in your life for a reason, season and lifetime. Don't be afraid of loving people from a distance. Stay grounded in God's word. Not gossip, pettiness or negativity. Cut anyone who brings that into your life.

In this stage of your life you can't afford to be around people that are trying to hold you to the old you. If they can't see that you are new and improved, let them go!

Once you know whose you are (God's child) and who you are (your identity), God will take it from there. Remember to tell your story even in the process of building your house. People need to see your transformation and hear about it, too. Your story is never for you! Tell your story so others are comfortable to live their truth.

Step 4: God's Vision for Your Life (The Layout Plan). This step requires you to be still and listen. God is not going to yell at you and He's not going to fight for you to hear his voice. God will whisper to you in a still small voice to advise you of you next step. I usually write down what He asks of me. So, I can go back and refer to it. I also ask

God to place a Bible verse on my heart to confirm his words. This works for me for where I am currently at in my walk and it gives me validation it was God's voice and not mine.

Write what God assigns to you with a date on it so you can go back to refer to them when everything comes to pass. Once He tells you something don't expect it to happen right away. It may take days, months or years to come to pass. We are on God's time. Once He tells you what He wants you to do, ask yourself:

Am I position to handle all that God has for me?
How's my heart? Is it in the right position?
How is my spiritual connection? It is strong enough?
Do I have the right people in my corner to walk with me?

If the answer is "Yes" to all those questions you are ready for step 5. If the answer is "No," pray about what you need.

Step 5: Strategizing (Installing). A dream is just a dream without any action attached to it. Strategize to create goals, to-do list, deadlines, and accountability. Your accountability partners will check to see if you are doing the things you said you would do. You may be thinking *"How do I create my strategy?* Let me put it into perspective for you. Here's how I broke down my goals:

Long Term Goals	One Year
Short Term Goals	6 months
Quarterly Goals	Every 3 months
1ˢᵗ Quarter Goals	January, February, March
2ⁿᵈ Quarter Goals	April, May, June
3ʳᵈ Quarter Goals	July, August, September
4ᵗʰ Quarter Goals	October, November, December

Monthly Goals	Each month
Micro Goals	Daily

This helped me strategize. If you try this and it doesn't work for you, pray about it. Ask God how he wants you to strategize. Don't get upset when your goals don't go as planned. Try to get it done next month.

Don't give up on it.

Giving up is the easiest thing.

Maybe the timing isn't right.

Each step helps you prepare for what God has in store for you.

Create a list of goals each month.

Compare it to the last month's list.

Place your goals in a place where you can see them to keep your memory refreshed.

Once God gives you the vision, He will supply you with the resources, connections, and finances. Speaking of finances this is going to require you to do some saving!

Do not save what's left after spending but spend what is left after saving! – Warren Buffett

By you saving, you are funding your dreams. God will see you working towards your goal and He will step in and interfere. He also wants to see what you can do. Faith without work is dead. This is where consistency and discipline kicks in. If you don't have it right now, it's ok. Start working toward it. It's something you develop overtime. It doesn't just come overnight. So you may have to switch up your daily ritual to incorporate your goals into your schedule.

I hope this isn't too much information to take in. I just really want you to be the best version of you. Realize everything you want in life is obtainable. You must pray, plan, pray, work and manifest it into the Universe.

Step 6: Execute (Tidying Up). It's time to put action behind everything you want to do. It's time to watch your plan unfold right before your eyes.

You can't play any games.

You have to be willing to run your own race.

You must be in competition with yourself.

Each day is a chance to be better than the person you were yesterday.

Don't look around or you will miss what's on your plate.

Look within to know you have what it takes.

You can't be scared to make mistakes.

They are created to teach you.

As time goes by and as you grow you will learn more about yourself.

It's time to apply all you know to give Birth to that ***PURPOSE MASTER PLAN***.

Take everything you got in you and make it work.

Life is about ***WALKING WITH A PURPOSE not WALKING ON PURPOSE***.

ACKNOWLEDGEMENTS

I am grateful for several people for their words of encouragement, wisdom, time and effort that went into this project. It didn't happen overnight but we made it happen.

First, I want to start by thanking God. This book was His plan. Without Him giving me this vision this project would have never came to life. Then I give thanks to the backbone of the family my Grandmother and Grandfather Brenda Scott and Henry Marsh. I remember telling my grandmother all my God-given dreams and how I was going to write this book. I told her it was going to impact the generations that came after me. She listened to me, she believed in me, each time I had a speaking event she prayed with me. Her eyes would light up every time I told her good news about my new beginnings. My Grandfather, a hardworking man, set the bar so high for me. Thank you for always being the male role I needed in my life. Thank you for spoiling me. I will never forget the day you ask me *"Do you know why I have no problem with spoiling you? Because you don't mind getting it on your own and that is what I love most about you."*

Julia Scott, thank you. My mother encourages me to keep going no matter what! She gives me life and also spoke life into me! When I told her my ideas, my dreams and my visions she never thought I was crazy, or I wasn't going to obtain them. She would always tell me that I was chosen. She always told me I was determined and I have always pushed myself to the limit. When I would get down, she would tell me stop being so hard on myself. She gives me strength in my weakness.

My son, **August Kirk**, is my reason. I always remind myself that I am setting an example for him if not for anyone else. I am showing him what it looks like to live out your God-given dream with some Faith, Prayer, and Planning. My sisters Latroya Corbin and Donae Lorwy thank you for always supporting me in anything I do. Thank you for being my #1 cheerleaders. Thank you for always begin a listening ear and here in my corner. My sisters are my first friends and I couldn't think of anyone else I would rather do life with than these two women. My only Nephew David Drewery. I love y'all. My father Philip Corbin for rebuilding with me and staying connected to me and installing wisdom in me at a young age that I carried throughout life with me. My big brother, Philip Bulls, thank you for always correcting my writing and letting me know where to place a comma or put a period. My little brother, D'Avay. Thanks to my grandmother, Martha Corbin, for believing in me always speaking so highly of me never holding your tongue and being so classy and such a lady. Thanks to my Uncle Ran and my Uncle Henry "Smoke" for being listening ears always.

A special thank you to my spiritual mentor Alison Nicole Wesley "Ms. Coco." Thank you for all you poured into me and seeing my spiritual gifts before I saw them! God knew I needed you. Thank to my Editor Rita Olds. Girl you've done a work in me. I'm so grateful for you seeing me properly and showing up for me! Thank you for keeping me flowing from one stage of this book to the next.

Thank you to a host of cousins and friends. I love you guys thank you all for being there for me when nobody was and supporting me, staying down with my vision even when it wasn't visible!

THANK YOU

I pray that your hearts will be flooded with light so that you can understand the confident hope he has given to those he called—his holy people who are his rich and glorious inheritance.Ephesians 1:18 NLT

We all have potential and purpose. Don't be in such a rush to tap into it that you end up in the wrong line of business! What's for you will always be there for you. Remember God is waiting on you! Say yes to his calling and will over your life so you can get this thing right! The sooner the better but remember it's never too late to begin again. Don't count yourself out God have plans for you and with his plans you will win!

Thank you to everyone that purchase my book. Thank you for investing into my dreams. I am so grateful for everyone. I pray the tools in this book you use it wisely and apply it to your life over and over again. Never forget the secret weapon YOU!!!! You have to believe in you and give you all of you to make the vision that God is giving you to come true.

Made in the USA
Middletown, DE
30 December 2019